D0764990

Contents

Introduction

When I first considered investing in gold, I confess that I knew very little about it. I was, however, intrigued enough to approach the idea with an open mind. That has long been my style of working, in a career spent as a serial entrepreneur, where I have invested in, and mentored, numerous start-up businesses with the potential for high growth. I have learned through experience that not everything is as it first seems. There is no substitute for the true, solid and valuable knowledge that always comes from diving in and getting to know what you are dealing with. I needed to do my homework about gold before I could make up my mind.

Once I began to explore the potential for gold something that immediately grabbed my attention was the fact that this precious commodity always seemed to receive very mixed reports. A quick search of the internet uncovered many investors who swear by gold as a sound investment. 'It is a crucial part of a diverse, balanced portfolio', the pro-gold crowd said, and, more importantly, the *only* foolproof hedge against inflation and economic downturns. Equally, many investors present a long list of 'sound reasons' why one should definitely not buy gold. 'It's impossible to value', is a common refrain. 'You have no true idea how it will fare in a downturn', is another assertion from those who refuse to believe it could ever be a sensible hedge against inflation or a weak US dollar. One of the most common rebukes for gold appears to be that it produces no income. If the detractor really wants to make a condescending point, they call gold a relic, with no place in the modern monetary system.

Finding enough respected investors who seem passionate about the strong value of gold, I resolved to persevere with my research and dig deeper to find answers to all my questions. After spending a lot of time trawling internet sites, both those *for* investing in gold and those *against*, I turned to the printed page. I read any book I could get my hands on that tackled the subject; some of them were helpful and some were not. A great deal of what I read was irrelevant since many books focus on exchange-traded funds and derivatives. In other words, they examine ways to invest in gold rather than tackling the pros and cons of investing in gold. I realised that to understand everything I needed to know, I needed a practical guide to determine what is behind the present and future value of gold. I wanted to delve more deeply into how gold has fared in the past against other types of investment. Equally importantly, if not more so, I wanted to get a feel for how it might perform in the future. Unfortunately, there are few books out there that serve this purpose, or that present the argument in a way that is succinct and easy to understand.

By this stage, I was certain of one thing: the pro-gold investment community were on to something. I was convinced enough to resolve to become a serious investor, perhaps more. There could, I decided, be a huge business opportunity for me in gold. It was at this point that I also decided that I would write the book I could have done with in the first place, when I first started to consider the potential of gold. That book is the one you are holding now.

The title of this book, *Gold Rush 2020: Why the time to invest in gold is right now*, shows how strongly I have come down on the side of the pro-gold investors. Having invested in gold for some time, I am now more convinced than ever that my initial instincts were correct: this is a huge and important opportunity.

Learning about gold has been fascinating, and I have shared many of my findings in this book. One thing I realised very quickly was that it is hard to get definitive views about gold because a great many people have a vested interest in saying (very loudly) that gold is a crazy investment. If these naysayers also work in Wall Street and the City, they belong to a long line of investors, analysts and advisors who have done well for themselves by telling us where to put our money. 'Put your hard-earned cash into stocks and shares, or bonds, and let it work for you,' they say. 'Sure, the market will go down, as well as up, but as long as you stay the course, you'll be quids, or dollars, in.' Much less is said about the handsome commission they get on our investments, which the "account statements" and "transaction summaries" are often less than clear about. In fact, some financial instruments are so complex, that the City whiz kids do not always understand them – as the financial meltdown of 2008–9 showed. Remember, they get these fees whether or not your investment actually realises any profits. 'Stick with it, the markets will return to health', they soothe. But what happens while you are waiting? Are your investments safe? Perhaps they are, perhaps not; but no one ever seems to want to discuss that.

Once I realised that I had to ignore the loud noises directing me away from gold, things became a little easier. I was able to examine its history and track how the precious metal has performed over many years. The more I learned about the value of gold, the more convinced

I became that I was on the right track. Gold is (one of) the most effective hedges against a downturn. This has been proved time and again.

If you are a keen market-watcher, you will realise that setting yourself up to be resilient against market movements is more important today than it has been for a decade or more, or perhaps ever. The economic environment is on the brink of a substantial change. While most people may think we have been riding the wave of prosperity for so long that it will inevitably go on for ever, nothing could be further from the truth. We have experienced a ten-year bull market – the S&P 500 Index rose from 666 to 2992 between March 2009 and Sept 2019 – but it is completely unsustainable, not to say built on an entirely false premise. While stock prices are soaring, there has been virtually no real growth in the companies connected with them. The world is sitting on a bubble of debt, and that bubble is about to burst in a very messy way, very soon. Despite all the vows about lessons learned following the global credit crunch of 2008/9, I wonder how far practices in Wall Street and the City have changed.

Sadly, it is the same with our ruling bodies. Their need to keep borrowing more and more requires governments to continually prop up the world's increasingly shaky financial systems in any way possible. Global debt stood at more than $246 trillion in the first quarter of 2019 according to the Institute of International Finance, up 50% from a decade ago. Yet printing more and more money, or tinkering with currency measures, is just meddling, and not very skilful meddling at that. It has created massive and damaging distortions to the markets, and to economies as a whole. In fact, very often the response of the authorities is the equivalent of loading everything onto a credit card and trying not to think too much about it. Sooner or later, though such policies will have real consequences. It is not a case of *if*, but *when*.

Who will suffer the most when the world enters the next recession, which most experts predict will hit by the second half of 2020? Ordinary savers, investors and retirees, of course, plus the millions of people who will lose their jobs, businesses and even homes. The 'clever' few on Wall Street and in the City know full well that too much money is chasing too few assets, but why slam on the brakes when there is still so much money to be made? Our central banks know it too, but find it easier to keep tinkering, for example printing money, rather than acknowledge the horrendous position they have helped push us all into.

As happens so often, the only way to ensure that you come out of an economic downturn unscathed is to look after yourself and your own interests. At times like these, when the global economy is on the brink of another significant crisis and financial assets are already showing signs of collapse, the only safe investment is gold. Gold's reputation as a safe haven in tough times is well earned because it held its value when everything else began to crash down around it. Gold has consistently performed best in an environment of high inflation, or debt, or when over-inflated stocks finally had their day of reckoning.

Investors would be well advised to ignore the negative noises about gold from Wall Street, whose traders have a vested interest in cajoling you to trade with them. No one should wait until a downturn sinks their wealth without trace. Smart investors should turn their assets into gold.

Today, gold's place in our financial system has become more important than ever. This book aims to explain how. Welcome to *Gold Rush 2020*.

ONE

Global Economic Outlook: The Only Thing That's Certain Is Uncertainty

The global economic outlook is shifting. Successive financial experts have warned that we are heading for the weakest economic performance since the worldwide financial crisis of 2008/9. If their voices have not been loud enough to cut through all the noise, or the credit crunch is not fresh in your mind, let me remind you of how bad things got in that last downturn. In one of what was easily the scariest periods of modern economic history, house prices fell by 16%[1] and share prices plunged at record-breaking rates. The Dow Jones Industrial Average lost 34% of its value[2] and the London Stock Market saw £90 billion wiped off the value of large companies in a single day.[3] In the subsequent mess, governments across the globe spent *tens of billions* on bank bailouts and in buying up bank shares, and millions of jobs were lost.[4]

If you think that years of enforced austerity have made all those problems go away: think again. We are currently sitting on top of global debt totalling $247 trillion.[5] The number is so large it is almost unimaginable. Global debt was soaring even before the financial crisis. As a share of world economy, the increase has mushroomed from an already alarming 2.48

1   http://news.bbc.co.uk/1/hi/business/7812108.stm
2   https://money.cnn.com/2008/12/31/markets/markets
    _newyork
3   www.theguardian.com/business/2008/dec/28/markets
    -credit-crunch-banking-2008
4   www.telegraph.co.uk/finance/jobs/7066404/1.3m-people
    -have-lost-their-jobs-in-the-recession-finds-report.html
5   Institute of International Finance figures, www.iif.com
    /Research/Capital-Flows-and-Debt/Global-Debt-Monitor

times gross domestic product (GDP) in 2003, to 3.18 times GDP in 2018.[6] In the first quarter of 2018, a further $8 trillion was heaped onto global debt.[6]

What is worrying analysts is that so much in our money markets is interdependent: many use the term 'house of cards'. Our economic systems are incredibly fragile. If one element fails or underperforms, it can easily upset the balance of others, leading to a loss of confidence and a dangerous spiral.

Threats to stability

Take, as an example, that $247 trillion of debt. The system is only sustainable because no one thinks about the implications too deeply. Households, businesses and governments alike are able to carry on because they can roll their portion of that debt over into new loans. That's

---

6   www.washingtonpost.com/opinions/the-247-trillion
     -global-debt-bomb/2018/07/15/64c5bbaa-86c2-11e8-8f6c
     -46cb43e3f306_story.html

right: they never really think about paying back what they have borrowed. This state of affairs only works while incomes and the economy as a whole *grow* fast enough to make the debt bearable, or to justify new loans. However, if the economy falters, or interest rates start to rise, or indeed anything discourages borrowers from paying their debts, a financial crisis can quickly escalate. Householders find credit unavailable; bailiffs are sent in; businesses start to close when they are not paid; people lose their jobs; governments can no longer raise what they need through taxation; when they try to borrow they find that they cannot afford the only terms available. When debt growth is no longer sustainable, lending slows or stops. Borrowers have to devote more of their cash flow to servicing existing debts, choking off the money available to spend on goods or services.

What is most frightening is that debt is not the only element of the economy that presents a risk to stability (although the scenario I've outlined should keep world leaders awake at night). There is, in fact, a long list of danger signs, each as worrying as the last. Taken individually, they could cause a significant dent in global confidence. Together, they could spell catastrophe.

The uncertain political climate is certainly another of the most obvious danger signals. There has been a very definite swing towards protectionist policies among governments across the globe. The introduction of trade tariffs against China by the USA, which were then extended to regions such as Europe, have rightly spooked many markets. Shortly after the first tranche of tariffs were announced, the International Monetary Fund (IMF) swiftly reduced the growth forecasts in its World Economic Outlook (WEO) for 2019 and 2020.[7] It had already reduced these forecasts in response to the stalling of global economic momentum thanks to weaker financial performances across the world. Negative impacts on car sales from new car emission standards in Germany,[8] as well as sovereign and financial risks dampening

---

7   World Economic Outlook, July 2019
8   www.ft.com/content/59074af2-cdff-11e8-b276
     -b9069bde0956

domestic demand in Italy[9] and a contraction in the Turkish economy,[10] have all hit harder than expected. Since tariffs were first mooted by President Trump, the trend towards tit-for-tat tariff wars shows no obvious signs of abating. Calls for calm and for countries to move quickly to solve their trade disagreements are going unheeded. The resulting uncertainty is already having an impact, with no sign of a resolution in sight.

On an individual, country-by-country basis, high-profile political challenges are also setting off alarm bells. In the UK, the prolonged Brexit process has seen the Bank of England repeatedly cut growth forecasts and shorten the odds on the country being plunged into a deep recession.[11] Analysts are also predicting that the fall-out from Brexit will have a negative impact on other Eurozone countries, and in particular

---

9   www.coface.com/Economic-Studies-and-Country-Risks /Italy

10   https://uk.reuters.com/article/us-turkey-economy-poll /turkeys-economy-to-contract-in-2019-limited-growth -ahead-reuters-poll-idUKKCN1UCoZ6

11   https://uk.reuters.com/article/uk-britain-boe/bank-of -england-cuts-growth-forecasts-as-brexit-and-global -worries-mount-idUKKCN1UR4C6

Germany which has already seen a slowdown in in its economy.[12] In France, a long series of bitter anti-government street protests by the so-called *gilets jaunes* (yellow vests) have been dubbed a 'catastrophe' for France's economy by the French finance minister Bruno Le Maire.[13]

All eyes are constantly on China, as an increasingly important global financial power, which is now at risk of a deeper-than-envisaged slowdown. Prior to the impact of the US trade war, the Chinese economy had already been slowing thanks to a range of factors including regulatory tightening and reduced public investment. We have already had a brief glimpse of how far-reaching the consequences of this loss of momentum can be. In 2015/16, concerns about the health of China's economy triggered abrupt and extensive sell-offs in the financial and commodity markets, which in turn put trading partners, commodity exporters and

---

12 https://uk.reuters.com/article/us-germany-economy -exports-analysis/its-brexit-not-trump-germanys-export -slump-mainly-caused-by-britain-idUKKCN1VI1IU

13 www.bbc.co.uk/news/world-europe-46499996

other emerging markets under huge pressure.[14] A repeat of this, but on a larger scale, would be more than catastrophic for the global economic outlook.

An optimist might like to think, or perhaps hope that, if all else fails, at least our respective governments have got it covered. Apologies: they have not. In fact, thanks to their misguided meddling in the markets in a desperate bid to smooth out any peaks and troughs and see off any financial crises, they have actually made matters worse. Thanks to the policies put in place after 2008/9, our leaders have done the equivalent of kicking the ball into the long grass, for someone to deal with later. The trouble is, we're getting very close to finding that ball.

---

14   www.nytimes.com/2016/01/10/business/international
      /chinas-hunger-for-commodities-wanes-and-pain
      -spreads-among-producers.html

Quantitative easing (QE)

This term came into widespread consciousness in the months and years that followed the credit crunch. This is where central banks purchase assets in order to stimulate the economy. It is a mechanism that is traditionally used when other policies, such as cutting interest rates, fail. Essentially, it involves 'buying bonds' from the government, and then depositing the proceeds back in the government's funds. In the book *Gold is a Better Way* by Adam Baratta,[15] the author compared the policy to a magic trick not unlike 'taking money from your left pocket and putting it in your right pocket'. It is not a particularly entertaining trick, but it certainly appears to have kept our governments amused. Between 2008 and 2016, the Federal Reserve in the USA printed $12.3 trillion;[16] while, in the UK, the Bank of England has spent £435 billion on buying government debt in a programme of QE.[17]

---

15 Morgan James Publishing, reprint 2019.
16 www.cnbc.com/2016/06/13/12-trillion-of-qe-and-the
    -lowest-rates-in-5000-years-for-this.html
17 www.bankofengland.co.uk/monetary-policy
    /quantitative-easing

The big issue is that QE is a bit of a blunt instrument, particularly when used for a prolonged period. Every time you add a dollar or pound to the economy by 'printing money', it devalues what is already in circulation. Virtually all of the money that has been printed has gone to the stock market, artificially inflating stock prices at a tremendous rate. The crazy thing is that QE can even have the opposite effect to what was intended. If central banks decide to use the extra funds to increase the capital reserves in their loan portfolio, rather than passing on reduced rates to their customers (ie the government, the public sector and – very occasionally – other banks), the benefit does not get realised. Governments cannot force banks to lend to anyone. Generally, it is the more well off that benefit by being able to borrow at lower rates. However, leaving 'average citizens' behind is always a dangerous strategy. Sooner or later there will be a need for a correction and this could easily be prompted by social unrest. Again, this is something that signals danger in an already uncertain climate. Or, at least it should, were anyone listening properly.

Inflation is the other big factor to watch as a result of QE. Inundating the economy with money means governments can keep interest rates artificially low, which in turn encourages consumers to spend more money. Sooner or later, though, it is inevitable that prices will begin creeping up, as supply is outstripped by demand. If prices start to inflate, it will force a hike in interest rates. Remember that $247 trillion in debt? Well, clearly a rise in interest rates would be a very worrying development indeed because it would drive up borrowing costs and make the debt system unsustainable. Do you see what I mean about the dangers of government meddling?

Despite the best efforts of governments to dampen things down, inflation is already on the rise. Food prices have been creeping northwards, oil prices are up and various other goods and services are costing noticeably more. In some countries, prices have increased by 15% over the past decade.[18] This means our purchas-

18   www.ourworldindata.org/food-prices

ing power is decreasing dramatically, which in turn is having a noticeable effect on standards of living. Once inflation reaches a certain level, it can wreck business competitiveness, particularly in the export market. If one country has a higher rate of inflation than others for a sustained period, its exports will be less price-competitive. This will reduce export orders, lower profits and threaten jobs. This, in turn, reduces a country's trade balance, which has a cumulative effect, accelerating falls in national income and employment. Once inflation starts to spiral, it is difficult to stop and can easily spill over into hyper-inflation, as we saw in Zimbabwe in 2006, where the official inflation rate surged to an astonishing 231,000,000%.[19]

Son of QE: QT

If QE was not worrying enough, we now have its successor, Quantitative Tightening (QT), to contend with. This is the brainchild of central banks that wish to begin unwinding their

---

[19] www.theguardian.com/world/2008/oct/09/zimbabwe

balance sheets, which have been artificially inflated thanks to QE. QT tightens the money supply in order to allow interest rates to rise. Instead of buying assets from the Treasury, central banks dump the assets they bought under QE back on the market. It is a process that will inevitably have a destabilising effect. If the stock market dives, as it is expected to, some borrowers will default.

But what of the City and Wall Street then? Surely they learned the lessons of 2008/9, which saw so many banks take such a spectacular and shocking fall from grace? Perhaps you will not be surprised to hear that financial institutions have sailed on with barely a backward glance at their fallen comrades, or the people that suffered as a result of their recklessness. More than ten years on from the Global Credit Crunch, there is ample evidence that lessons have not been learned. The banks that were deemed 'too big to fail' in 2008 are even bigger today than they were then. So are their derivative books. Stock markets are still massively over-hyped, with stock indices in the USA and across the western world repeatedly hitting all-time highs. This, in part, has been helped by QE, since so much of the virtual money that has been created has found its way into global stock markets, sending equity prices sky-high.

The gambling dens that are our major stock markets still thrive on the absurd theory that 'bad news is good news'. In other words, whenever economic numbers start to look weak (as they are doing at the moment), central banks step in and turn up the funny money dial that is QE – perhaps they will repackage QE in some other form. More money for equities! Forget about sensible indicators such as economic growth, or actual corporate performance: it's all about driving stock prices. This is how stocks continue to soar, despite dire warnings of weak economic fundamentals.

Other worrying signs

Perhaps even more worrying is the number of investors that are piling into direct-lending funds which specialise in borrowers who are too small, or too risky, to be bank clients. Here, borrowers are matched up with potential lenders, usually online. The practice, which began guardedly after the credit crunch, has now exploded into a financial sector all of its own, which is rapidly approaching a value of $1 trillion.[20] Money is streaming in from pension funds, insurers and hedge funds. Instead of throwing cash at big corporations, this lending boom is aimed at small, regional businesses. What worries experts is that in the search for anything that pays a decent return, investors are pouring money into all sorts of risky assets. Why? One word; yield. After a decade of QE and other central bank stimuli, yield from traditional sources such as the debt of blue chip corporations has started to look unattractive. If everything goes well, loans from private lenders to small businesses can be more lucrative than those to large companies. Yields of 7% to 9% per annum are being touted. This is fine while repayments are made, but when

---

20   https://www.wsj.com/articles/too-much-money-is
     -a-worry-for-direct-lenders-1539179967

they dry up there often is no underlying asset value (ie nothing for the 'fire sale'). Oh, and remember those collateralised debt obligations that caused all the fuss around 2008/9? Well, they are back. Wall Street has homed in on direct-lending funds and issued almost $20 billion of collateralised loan obligations,[21] slicing up risky loans into securities with respectable triple-A ratings. Again, we all remember where that magic trick ended last time.

Do not for one moment imagine the risks stop with the private lenders who put their money into direct lending. Many billions in credit lines are coming from banks, which in turn pass a portion of the debt on to their own yield-seeking investors, such as pension funds, endowments and sovereign wealth funds. These are, of course, the funds that affect each and every one of us. The risks for investors and the companies they invest in will grow when, inevitably, interest rates start to rise. Those risks will be even more acute for any firms

---

21 www.wsj.com/articles/junk-debt-sends-early-warning
    -signals-11568545201

that borrowed heavily in the good times. It is only once the cost of all that borrowing starts to rise that we will fully appreciate the extent of the damage, and that, as you have probably guessed by now, is going to be too late.

As if all these individual signs of a looming and devastating downturn are not bad enough, we are also stepping over the threshold of a massive demographic crisis. The baby boom generation – those born between 1946 and 1964 – are now at retirement age. Indeed, millions have already downed tools and headed off to tend their gardens, or paint their boats, or relax in the sun, all being well. In a disastrous set of circumstances, this enormous population bubble coincides with a time when the birth rate is at its lowest point ever. By 2030, those aged 65 and older will make up over 20% of the population.[22] That vastly top-heavy proportion will be even greater in some countries. This will have a devastating impact on the

---

22 www.ons.gov.uk/peoplepopulationandcommunity/birthsdeathsandmarriages/ageing/articles/livinglongerhowourpopulationischangingandwhyitmatters/2018-08-13

world's economy because, with fewer people of working age, wages will rise as employers fight to attract and retain the best from a smaller pool of labour. Economic growth will slow because it is so intrinsically linked with corporate profits. Any cut in company earnings will, in turn, erode returns for investors (who, as we have already seen, already face many inter-related economic threats). Meanwhile, just at a time when taxes will need to rise to pay for all the services retirees require, from pensions to healthcare, tax revenues from the working population will plummet. Just when you think it could not get worse, add to the mix the fact that spending in a retired household is 43% less than in households of those of working age.[23] Given that consumption accounts for a huge percentage of economic activity, this is poised to be a disastrous deflationary force.

There is more, too. According to a survey by global investment giant BlackRock,[24] the

---

23 www.prudentialplc.com/analysis/spending-habits-in-uk
    -retirement
24 www.blackrock.com/uk/intermediaries/insights
    /millienial-investors

average baby boomer has massively under-saved for their retirement. In America, this equates to a retirement fund of $136,000. Even assuming 7% returns on that pension pot (when in reality the figure is more like 2%),[25] this equates to an annual income of $9,000. With the average fees for a place in a retirement home at $45,000 per year, that is quite a shortfall. So, what do our retiring boomers do to guarantee their ongoing comfort and care? They sell their stocks and shares and retreat into the relative safety of bonds. Just pause for a second and consider what that means for the stock market. Nearly 40% of stock market equities are owned by retirement accounts. Any wave of forced selling will flood the market with billions of pounds/dollars of equities, to levels it is almost impossible to speculate about. With millions of baby boomer retirees poised to divest their portfolios in the coming years, when the market is at an all-time high, the outcome cannot be good. Savvy investors should already be thinking long and hard about exit strategies.

---

25 www.blackrock.com/uk/intermediaries/insights
/millienial-investors

There is no question about whether or not we are heading into financial crisis. None of the 'recovery' that supposedly happened after 2008/9 is a result of growth and productivity. Any perceived improvements in our situation have been produced through sleight of hand or financial engineering. Let us not forget that it was financial engineering that got us into the last major recession. Stocks and bonds have never been more inflated after a record-setting bull run and the markets have never been so distorted. Meanwhile property prices continue their apparently gravity-defying upward trajectory.

But what of gold, you might ask? Where does it sit within these worrying trends? And that is the interesting thing. While the prices of financial stocks have massively inflated, the prices of real tangible goods and commodities have not followed this pattern at all. In fact, they have deflated. Gold is down from highs of $1,900 per ounce, to a range between $1,350 and $1,500. Silver is also down from a high of $49 per ounce, to a level in the range of $15 to $17 per ounce. This is an odd correlation when you consider that, as credit tightens over the next few years, and the problems detailed here begin to impact, there will be massive and prolonged pressure on stocks and bonds. Governments and central banks cannot keep pumping more money in whenever the problem looks like getting out of control. It seems ever more likely that gold will have a key role to play in what happens next.

In the light of the threats we currently face, which are coming at us from all directions – over-inflated stocks, inflation, runaway direct lending, or a massive population imbalance – there seems to be one sensible solution. Anyone who is serious about maintaining their wealth and standard of living needs to build a solid defence against the downturn that will inevitably hit us when all of these over-inflated assets slump back to their true value. The solution is to find a safe haven for your money. In my mind the *only* safe haven worth having today is gold. In chapter two I will explain why.

TWO

Gold Is The Safe Haven

It's an investment fact-of-life that as we get older, we get more cautious. That goes doubly, even trebly, so when the dark clouds of market turmoil gather as they are doing today. But how do you protect what you have worked and saved so hard for? No one wants to see that wealth disappear. The answer is to find a safe haven.

In the past, when volatility struck, there were a number of defensive alternatives. Betting on the US dollar has long seemed like a good strategy, since the currency has been a solid part of international trade for decades. Likewise, government bonds have traditionally been a safe diversifier from equities when seeking to preserve wealth. And then, of course, there are so-called defensive stocks such as utilities, fast-moving consumer goods (FMCGs) and pharmaceuticals. The clue here is in the title, defensive stocks, because these are the investments that can generally be relied upon because people will always need them, so they provide constant dividend and stable earnings. Finally, there is gold, an investment that if held for the long term has been proved to outperform major equity markets many times over.

Choices, choices. With four solid options to pick from everything looks fine. All you need to do is commit and your wealth will be perfectly safe as the rest of the market descends into chaos. Right? Except this is not the case. As I have already highlighted, we are in the midst of an exceptional range of circumstances which are steadily converging and bringing us to the brink of market chaos. None of the normal rules apply any more. And that also goes for the way we defend ourselves. The traditional boltholes – the dollar, government bonds and defensive stocks – have lost their super-powers. If you rely on them to see you through, you will get badly burned.

Let me explain why.

Let us start with the Mighty Greenback, the US dollar. The dollar replaced the British pound as the world's premier reserve currency in 1945, as a result of the Bretton Woods agreements, formalising global acknowledgement of America as the leading world power in the wake of the Second World War. A reserve currency is a currency that is held in significant reserves by governments and institutions as a means of international payment and to support individual national currencies. Just to continue the history lesson for a moment, the original reserves used to include mostly gold and silver, but the Bretton Woods agreements expanded the acceptable reserves to include other currencies, of which the dollar is the premier one. Then, in 1971, President Richard Nixon pushed precious metals out of the picture altogether by barring all future major currencies from officially being converted into gold.

History lesson over. What's important to note here is that reserve currencies have always had a significant impact on monetary and trade policies around the globe. The fact that 60% of all foreign currency reserves in the world are in US dollars sounds pretty encouraging. It shores up the dollar's reputation as the dominant global currency and makes it sound as though things are stable and on an even keel. Scratch below the surface though, and the picture is not nearly so bright, and increasingly less so.

The Red Flag

Thanks to the respective size of their economies, the euro and the Japanese yen have become increasingly popular reserve currencies over time. In fact, Japan has quietly enjoyed the position of being the world's largest creditor for nearly three decades. But that is not the biggest red flag. That accolade belongs (if you will excuse the joke) to China which has been aggressively positioning itself as the next leading economic super-power for some time. China has been the largest contributor to world growth since the financial crash of 2008/9. It became a top global exporter in 2009 and claimed its spot as the largest trading nation in the world four years after that.[1] Beijing's $1 trillion Belt and Road Initiative (BRI) has been dubbed a Chinese Marshall Plan. The state-backed strategy for global dominance is both a stimulus package for a slowing economy and a massive marketing campaign for Chinese investment around the world. The 'belt' of over-land corridors and 'road' of maritime shipping lanes now stretch from south-east Asia, to eastern Europe, to Africa, spanning 71 countries that contain half of the world's population and account for a quarter of global GDP.

---

1 https://www.theguardian.com/business/2014/jan/10 /china-surpasses-us-world-largest-trading-nation

No one can have failed to notice the rise of China's economic power and reach. Indeed, the IMF named the Chinese yuan a global reserve currency in 2015.[2] Today, economists are tipping the Chinese economy to become *three times* larger than the US economy by 2040.[3] Hardly surprisingly, there are many in China, and indeed elsewhere, who are questioning why the dollar should continue to occupy a position that is so preeminent among reserve currencies. The problem for anyone that might be considering seeking a safe haven in the dollar is that such talk is not just taking place behind closed doors. There is increasing evidence that China and other emerging powers are making agreements to move away from the dollar in international trade.[4] The dollar is now nowhere near as supreme as many believe it to be. The issue of the flight from the dollar has been exacerbated by America's protectionist trade policies, which

2   https://uk.reuters.com/article/us-china-currency-imf
     /chinas-yuan-joins-elite-club-of-imf-reserve-currencies
     -idUKKCN1212WC

3   www.weforum.org/agenda/2016/12/the-world-s-top
     -economy-the-us-vs-china-in-five-charts

4   www.forbes.com/sites/charleswallace1/2018/08/14
     /are-russia-and-china-trying-to-kill-king-dollar/
     #66534f897948

have diverted trade away from the USA. When countries seek less onerous agreements with new trade partners, it makes more sense to settle the bill in the currencies concerned, rather than the dollar.

In the autumn of 2018, as the American trade war with China rumbled on, China signed a currency swap deal with Japan which was worth C¥200 billion (US$29 billion). At the same time, the Bank of China's Tokyo branch was named by the Japanese central bank as the clearing house for yuan transactions in Japan.[5] The deal, which was barely reported at the time and certainly stoically ignored by the US media, was hugely significant. Here we saw the world's second- and third-largest economies joining hands. They were not just agreeing to being able to exchange billions of yuan and yen either. The agreement also added much needed clout to Beijing's plan to increase the importance of the yuan on the world stage.

---

5   www.scmp.com/economy/china-economy/article
     /2170426/china-and-japan-sign-us29-billion-currency
     -swap-forge-closer

It's not just the Red Dragon that is breathing fire down the neck of the US dollar. Russia has also weighed in: it dumped $101 billion in US holdings from its reserves in 2018, shifting instead to euros and yuan. A further $21 billion was invested in the Japanese yen at the same time.[6] Only a year earlier, the dollar had accounted for nearly half of Russia's $430 billion of reserves. After the holdings dump, just 22% of Russian reserves were held in dollars.[7] At the same time, yuan holdings jumped to nearly 15% of those reserves, a share ten times the average for global central banks and a clear reflection of the change in sentiment towards the dollar. The Russian government has suggested that the 2018 move was in response to tough sanctions imposed by America and predicted that other countries such as Iran and Turkey, which are also buckling under the weight of US sanctions, might follow suit. Whatever the impetus, the outcome is the same. The days of the US dollar

---

6   www.themoscowtimes.com/2019/01/10/russia-dumps
      -101-billion-from-dollar-reserves-in-pivot-to-china-a64092

7   www.economist.com/finance-and-economics/2019/01/17
      /the-central-bank-of-russia-shifts-its-reserves-away-from
      -the-dollar

as the premier international reserve currency look increasingly numbered.

Even America's traditionally staunchest allies are questioning the dollar's dominance. In his 2018 annual program address, former European Commission President Jean-Claude Juncker told the European Parliament that it was 'absurd' that 80% of European energy imports were settled in dollars.[8] Like China, European policymakers are actively looking for opportunities to expand the role of their own currency, the euro.

Prospects for the dollar

What would happen, then, if the dollar lost its place as the major reserve currency? According to economic experts, two conditions need to be in place for the US dollar to collapse. The first is an ongoing, underlying weakness. Between

---

8   www.reuters.com/article/us-eu-juncker-euro
     /eus-juncker-wants-bigger-global-role-for-euro
     -idUSKCN1LS0BK

2002 and 2018, the dollar declined by 6% according to the US Dollar Index. This is largely due to US debt almost tripling from $6 trillion to $22 trillion over the same period. The debt-to-GDP ratio has consistently exceeded 100% and is constantly rising. Today it is more than 105%.[9] The second is that the strength of the dollar is based on its position as the major reserve currency. As this position is clearly slipping away, the dollar is looking less and less like a viable currency alternative for everyone to buy.

It is important to say now that it is hugely unlikely that the dollar will collapse. Countries that have the power to trigger that seismic shock, such as China, Japan and Russia, do not want this to happen. It is not in their best interests because they own trillions of dollars of US debt. If they dump their holdings of US Treasury notes, they would almost certainly cause a worldwide panic that would most likely impact their own currencies: a spectacular own goal. Likewise, international markets depend

---

9   https://tradingeconomics.com/united-states/government
     -debt-to-gdp

on US consumers, and it is always a daft strategy to bankrupt your best customer. However, while they do not want to blow up the US dollar entirely, these competitors are, without a doubt, chipping away at the Mighty Greenback's dominance. The dollar is in gradual decline and it is heading in only one direction. So, is the dollar viable as a potential safe haven? The market and general economic outlook say not.

Prospects for bonds

With the dollar most likely out of the picture, let us turn to the second defensive item on the list. What about government bonds? A bond documents a loan that the purchaser, or bondholder, makes to the bond issuer. Governments and corporations issue bonds when they need capital. When an investor buys a bond, they are lending the government or corporation money. Like any type of loan, that bond pays interest periodically and then repays the principal sum at a stated time, known as the maturity date. This is why traditional investment wisdom has always advocated holding bonds, as well as stocks, as part of a balanced portfolio. What could be more reliable and dependable than the government?

The accepted barometer for the government bond market is the yield on ten-year bonds. In recent times, the readings derived from that barometer have been at best variable, and at worst downright gloomy. In fact, bond yields are currently hitting record lows. In the UK, if you put your cash into one for ten years, the government will pay you just 79 pence a year for every £100 you lend it.[10] In Germany, investors have to *pay* the German government for the privilege of owning its bonds. And the bond yields are just 0.39% per annum.[11] Meanwhile, French ten-year bond yields have dropped to 0.065% and Belgian ten-year bond yields are below zero for the first time ever.[12] In the USA,

10   www.rock-wealth.co.uk/financial-strife

11   www.thelocal.de/20160713/germany-makes-investors -pay-interest-on-bonds

12   www.reuters.com/article/europe-bonds/update-2-record -lows-for-euro-zone-bond-yields-as-us-jobs-data-fuels -rate-cut-talk-idUSL8N23E3MB

the US benchmark 10-year Treasury bond is below 2% per annum.[13]

The background to this disappointing performance is the historical low level of interest rates. The underlying fundamental for bonds is interest rates. The explanation can be a little confusing. The higher the interest rate (or coupon), the lower the price, whereas when coupon rates are lower, bond prices are higher. A bond that pays out 6% per annum has a lower price than one that pays out 3%. Historically, the prime interest rate, or the rate at which banks lend to the public, has averaged around 7%.[14] Today, interest rates are at historical lows: they have averaged less than 3% per annum over the past decade. Often they have been far lower than that.[15]

As a result, there has never been a better time to borrow cash, hence the boom in debt. But for

---

13   www.cnbc.com/2019/08/15/us-bonds-30-year-treasury
     -yield-falls-below-2percent-for-first-time-ever.html
14   https://tradingeconomics.com/united-kingdom/bank
     -lending-rate
15   https://tradingeconomics.com/united-kingdom/interest
     -rate

the lender? Well, there is not much upside. And that goes for lending money to the government via bonds, too. Thanks to these low interest rates, bonds have never been more expensive. So, the price for protecting your cash via bonds is currently pretty high. You could even say that they are so costly and unreliable, they have lost the status of safe haven altogether.

But there is more to the bond story. Interest rates will not stay low for ever. At some point it is inevitable that they will rise (and that point gets closer by the day). The financial system cannot function forever on the current basis. If interest rates surge, bond prices will fall, which will be bad news for anyone holding bonds. Alan Greenspan, the former chairman of the US Federal Reserve, has been warning for months that the bond market is in a bubble and that this bubble is on the verge of popping.[16] In a spectacular double whammy, when interest rates rise, equity investors will also be punished if equities start to look expensive. This reduces

---

16   www.cnbc.com/2018/03/01/ex-fed-chair-greenspan-we
      -are-in-a-bond-market-bubble.html

the point of holding a balanced portfolio rather significantly. Whichever way you look at it, bonds do not offer the safe haven you might be seeking.

Prospects for defensive stocks

And so, to stocks. It's helpful to talk about stocks/equities generally, before turning specifically to defensive stocks. As all investors will be aware, stocks have been enjoying a ten-year bull market, the longest bull market in history. The stock market is said to be a 'bull market' when equity stock prices increase by 20% or more in a year. At the time of writing, The FT100 in the UK has more than doubled in value since March 2009, while the S&P 500 in the US has nearly quadrupled in the same period.[17] It's a global phenomenon too: German stocks have returned nearly 250% since the Credit Crunch and Chinese and Japanese stock markets are not far behind with returns of nearly 200%.

---

17   www.brewin.co.uk/charities/insight-for-charities/ten-years-after-the-financial-crisis

[18] So, a reasonably diverse portfolio is worth around three times what it was in 2008/9. Three times! Think about that for a moment. Now turn your attention to the companies listed on those markets that have seen their stock prices soar by 300%. The output of the companies listed on the markets has not risen by anything like that amount. Not even close. With the challenges we now face in global trade, most organisations struggle to get out of single-digit growth. Even so, the bull market thunders on, apparently unruffled by such encumbrances as matching share prices to the value of what is actually produced.

How over-valued is the market, though? Warren Buffet, the much-respected super-investor and so-called Sage of Omaha, has a very handy measurement. In his view, the single best way to assess stock valuations is to compare market capitalisation with GDP. The calculation, known as the Warren Buffett Indicator, takes the amount of cash invested in

---

18   www.schroders.com/en/insights/economics/the-longest
     -bull-market-in-history-in-five-charts

the stock market at any one time and then compares it to current GDP, expressing the result as a ratio. The reasoning behind the metric is that the large companies that make up the markets also contribute significant sums to GDP. After reviewing the ratio over time, Warren Buffet drew the following conclusions.

Where the total current value of the stock market is 70%–90% of GDP, stock prices are fair. If the total market capitalisation is less than 50% of GDP, stock prices are significantly undervalued. At the other end of the scale, if the total of all equities issued to investors times current stock prices is 115% of GDP, then the market is *significantly overvalued.* There is a handy calculator at www.goldisabetterway.com. When I did the exercise at the time of writing, the ratio was 145%. To put this into context, let me give you some other key dates when the stock market/GDP ratio was this much out of whack. It happened in the years 1929, 2000 and 2008. The historians amongst you will recognise the dates as, respectively, the start of the Great Depression, the bursting of the Dot Com Bubble and the Credit Crunch. The market cap v GDP ratios at these times were also at significant levels: 130%, 151% and 117%.[19]

Still not convinced that the stock market is a bit 'toppy'? Another measure for you to try out was devised by Robert Shiller, a Yale economist. He has focused on price-to-earnings ratios (P/E) as a way of eliminating the distractions caused by fluctuations in share prices, which can be skewed by short-term factors (market reports, gossip, rumours). Shiller's metric, known as CAPE Shiller (Cyclically Adjusted Price-to-Earnings) takes ten-year tranches of earnings, adjusts them for inflation and then calculates a fair price for that ten-year income stream. The model looks back as far as the beginning of the twentieth century and shows that the average historical CAPE Shiller is around 17 times earnings. If the current P/E ratio falls significantly below this, it is a sign that the market is significantly undervalued. This would signal that long-term gains could be exceptional. If, for example, you had invested at the low point in June 1982, when the CAPE Shiller ratio was

---

19   www.goldisabetterway.com

6, you would have been there for the start of a juicy 18-year bull run. Your investment would have grown to ten times its starting value.

Alternatively, let's turn to times when the P/E ratio has not been so attractive. At the peak of the Dot Com Bubble in 2000, the CAPE Shiller P/E score was 41. This large figure even eclipses Black Tuesday, 29 October 1929, when panicked sellers traded nearly 16 million shares on the New York Stock Exchange as share prices plummeted around them. The CAPE Shiller P/E then was 31. Immediately before the housing collapse that started the ball rolling on the 2008/9 financial crisis, the CAPE Shiller measure was 27. And today? At the time of writing, it sits at 28, but over the 18 months to August 2019 the CAPE Shiller P/E has been as high as 34. If you accept Professor Shiller's reasoning then, should you invest at current levels, you ought to expect extremely poor long-term performance in your portfolio. The key to investing is, after all, to buy low and sell high.

One of the most worrying aspects of current share price levels, particularly if you have one eye on what happened around the millennial Dot Com Bubble, is the boom in technology stocks. Tech stocks dominate the growing number of companies that trade at more than 10× their annual revenue. Facebook, for example, trades at 15× annual revenue. To show what this means, if Facebook did not spend one single dollar on anything, not wages, R&D, equipment updates, taxation, anything, and its annual revenue continued at the current level, it would take 15 years for investors to break even. This is, of course, an absurd scenario. It is as if you or I owned a shop making a respectable $40,000 a year in profit, after paying rent, wages and for all the stock, and pretended the shop was worth $600,000. Would you buy this shop for $600,000 if it was only bringing in $40,000 a year in profit? That would be a pretty daft investment. Yet if you own Facebook, Netflix (13×) or Google (9×), that is the sort of pay-back equation that you are banking on.

Ah, you may say, I am already on to this. I am only investing in *defensive* stocks. These are stocks in market sectors such as food, utilities, healthcare and non-durable goods such as soap and toothpaste, that are less vulnerable to downturns thanks to their non-cyclical nature. There's no boom and bust in defensive stocks: everyone always needs to eat, wash and keep the lights on. These industries have historically been relied upon to perform more evenly through good and bad economic times, with their stock prices remaining more stable and reliable. Except, in this case, I would need to refer you back to the beginning of this section on equities. That record-breaking bull run? The prices of defensive stocks have largely kept pace with those of other stocks. That makes them expensive.

Take Unilever as a case in point. Its shares are valued at a multiple of 22× the company's annual earnings. Reckitt Benckiser's P/E ratio has been as high as 29 in recent times, according to Bloomberg data.[20] These are all at the top end of their historical ranges. Commentators are already comparing the current situation to the historic scenario of 'the nifty fifty'. This nickname appeared in the 1970s, describing a group

---

20   www.bloomberg.com/quote/RB/:LN

of fifty large, consumer-focused stocks such as McDonalds, Disney and Polaroid, which were prized for their high growth. Unfortunately, their elevated and much discussed valuations encouraged investors to sell their stocks, which is exactly what happened, and the purchasers saw significant underperformance of the stocks through the 1980s.

If you spoke to anyone in Wall Street or the City, they would most likely say there are always merits to having high-quality stocks in defensive sectors. After all, they would reason, it seems unlikely that interest rates, or bond yields, will rise significantly anytime soon, given the broader concerns about the wider economy. Good companies are more than capable of growing dividends in the long run. They would most likely argue strongly against the 'nifty fifty' comparison, too; and, in fairness, the nifty fifty were trading on up to 50 × earnings. Defensives trading on up to 30 × earnings seems the norm in the current environment. Even so, it is not a good sign.

Taken in the context of everything else that has been said in this chapter, I would argue strongly with anyone who told me that it will all self-correct soon. It is utter madness to ignore the possibility that any correction will be substantial and will change the investing environment markedly. No self-correction is painless; but the shift downwards will more than likely earn its place in the rogues' gallery of painful corrections, such as the bursting of the Dot Com Bubble and the global Credit Crunch. History has shown us time and time again that boom times always, always end, and often badly. Every one of the twelve bull runs since the Great Depression in the 1930s did, eventually, end. The factors that brought each one to an end have varied, but the result has always been the same: over-confidence followed by panic. For some reason, though, investors usually seem to forget this. More worryingly, Wall Street and the City, who make their living by watching the markets so they can make recommendations to people like you and me, must be wilfully ignoring this tendency of history to repeat itself. A cynic might conclude that this is because they make big commissions on share sales so it is in their interest to look upon the 'bright' side.

The point to remember is this: holding onto over-priced assets is not a defensive strategy. It is, in fact, the polar opposite. Likewise betting on the dollar when the dollar is under attack or relying on government bonds when interest rates are so low and will have to adjust, sooner or later. There is only one true defensive play right now; only one true safe haven: gold. The reason you should be turning to gold is because, right now, it is the only asset that can be trusted to store value. Once again, history shows this: during the 2008 global financial crisis, when the Dow Jones index plummeted from 14,000 to 7,000, and $10 trillion dollars was wiped off global stock markets, the gold price rose from $850 per Troy ounce to $1,900 per Troy ounce; an impressive 131% increase in value.[21]

But there is a lot more to gold. In chapter 3 I will show you why gold is such a smart investment when confidence in the financial system is low. At times like these the value of gold *always* increases.

---

21   www.moneymetals.com/precious-metals-charts/gold -price

THREE

Rare, Reliable And Dependable – Gold Holds Its Value

If you are an experienced investor and you've read this far, thank you. I know that much of what I have written will most likely go against everything you have ever been told about investing. The party line is: stay the course. Put your money into a good, balanced portfolio of equities and bonds and let it work for you. Invest in your future and it will work out well. If gold is ever mentioned, it is usually as a warning: *don't invest in gold!* Try to probe in more depth for a reason and the response will inevitably be something along the following lines: gold does not *do anything.* You buy it and it just sits there. It does not pay any interest, or dividends. In fact, it costs you money because you have to store it and insure it. Where is the upside?

The starting point in my argument in favour of gold is to turn the questions the naysayers always ask on their head and ask: where is the *downside?* Yes, it is true that gold does not pay any income while you hold it, like stocks and bonds do (or fail to do – please see chapter 2). But there is one major risk that all the other assets discussed here run, but gold does not: all the other investments carry a real risk of a *permanent* loss of value.

To break this down further, let's say you placed £1,000 of your money in the bank, or used it to buy shares. In this scenario, the value of your holding is the amount you get back when you come to withdraw your investment. Your stake has become the liability of the bank or company whose shares you hold. You are their creditor.

If that organisation turns around and says: 'I am very sorry, we cannot pay our creditors', then the value of that £1,000 is destroyed. To be sure, the price of gold can go down as well as up, but the elemental and solid nature of gold is its greatest asset. If you own an ounce of gold today, you will own one tomorrow, as long as you do not sell it or pass it on. No one can take that away from you.

Gold has been as a medium of exchange for centuries thanks to its intrinsic properties. It has been used in jewellery, dentistry and, most recently, in electronics. Whatever happens economically, it should always be in demand – at some level. There are plenty of other reasons why gold has been in favour as a currency since as far back as 550 BC when King Croesus minted coins in what is now modern-day Turkey.[1] Gold can be divided into any smaller unit, without losing any of its value, unlike diamonds. It is also difficult to counterfeit. There is a limited stock of gold. To date, 166,500 tonnes of the

---

1   www.cityam.com/short-history-investing-gold-and
     -expect-2017

precious metal have been mined throughout history,[2] which, although it sounds a lot, is only enough to fill an Olympic-sized swimming pool. Only a further 2,500 tonnes are added to the stock each year. This rarity reinforces its value.

Something else that adds to the attraction of gold is that it is incorruptible: it does not tarnish or break down. When gold was the predominant unit of currency, inflation could only ever be linked to the speed of getting it out of the ground since there is only so much new gold available at any one time. This is a somewhat different scenario to that of paper money, which is notoriously vulnerable to government actions: we discussed quantitative easing in chapter 1, which can and does lead on to new problems such as inflation. Governments cannot magically expand the gold supply, as they have so often done with money.

2   www.visualcapitalist.com/12-stunning-visualizations-of
     -gold-bars-show-its-rarity

The gold standard

Hardly surprisingly, the history of gold as a currency has had its ups and downs. A high point for gold was certainly when, after centuries of being traded, its status as an important asset in finance was cemented by the adoption of the gold standard, firstly by England in 1819, then by France, Germany, Switzerland, Belgium and the United States. The gold standard meant that the currencies of those countries were pegged to the gold price. It happened at a time of growing global trade and the parity rates were handy when pricing international transactions. As time went on, other countries joined the standard, as it was a useful way to gain access to the newly industrialised markets.

As global trade expanded, eventually the gold standard slowly began to erode. A succession of governments, along with their central banks, came to the conclusion that maintaining monopoly privileges over the supply of their national currencies was preferable to tying the supply and value of their currencies to the price and availability of gold, which they saw as an unhelpful restraint on fiscal policy. Governments wanted the ability to increase the money supply at times of economic strife, to ease pressure on markets and see off any sudden drops or worrying surges. The gold standard did not make this interference easy. At the same time, there began to be concerns that gold producing nations were at an unfair advantage over those who do not produce the precious metals. The conclusion? Many analysts began to argue strongly that gold was too inflexible to take a place at the centre of national economies.

Over the years, the gold standard was occasionally suspended when various ruling parties found themselves spending considerably more than their gold reserves could cover. This was a particular problem during wartime and, of course, the twentieth century saw two World Wars. Nations were also experiencing increasing struggles in their efforts to peg the value of their national currencies to gold, without creating distortions. Gold's price does change, after all. Something had to give and it was the gold standard. As mentioned in chapter 2, in the Bretton Woods agreements after the Second World War the Allied countries accepted the dollar as the premier reserve as opposed to gold, and, in return, the US government pledged to keep enough gold to back its dollars. Gold's status was further eroded in 1971, when President Nixon dropped the guarantee to back the dollar with gold, making the dollar fiat currency.[3] Fiat currencies move freely against each other; fiat currency is usually paper money and is not backed or guaranteed by a commodity. Its *value* is decided by a central authority, which tries to guarantee this and distribute the currency accordingly; but its value might drift out of line with its *price*, which is decided by the markets. By eliminating any connection at all with gold, the US dollar became another piece of paper. Its value has decreased by 92% since 1913.[4]

---

3   www.federalreservehistory.org/essays/gold _convertibility_ends

4   https://kinesis.money/case-studies/paper-money -eventually-returns-to-its-intrinsic-value-zero

Gold vs. fiat currencies

All of which brings me neatly to the next plus point for gold: reliability. Considered from this viewpoint, it is difficult to see why the paper alternative has become so popular. Fiat currencies have been around since the time of the Romans and their history has been littered with failures. In fact, a study of 775 fiat currencies by Dollardaze.org found that there is *not one single* historical example of a fiat currency holding its value. They have been monetarily reformed (24%), still in circulation, awaiting outcome (23%), destroyed by war (21%), failed through inflation (20%) or destroyed by independence (12%).[5] It's hardly an inspiring record.

The innate problem with fiat currencies is that they are based on a coercive, rather than a voluntary, market relationship. A central bank is tasked with keeping things in check and will seek unfettered control in order to see off

---

5   www.dinardirham.com/the-rise-and-fall-of-fiat -currencies

threats from competing currencies. Unfortunately, governments are not run by all-knowing, infallible, selfless individuals who consistently make financial and economic decisions for the good of the whole of the population. Even if government offices were staffed with financial geniuses, the most careful and prudent planning can unleash unintended consequences requiring further interventions. This has unquestionably been the case with QE and QT, as discussed in chapter 1.

To see how this might impact your wealth, let's take the dollar, since it is still quite closely related to gold. Every dollar bill has three words printed on it: *Federal Reserve Note.* The word 'note' indicates that it is a debt, or an obligation, or a promise. The Federal Reserve is backing that dollar. If you have one in your wallet, it is backed by your faith in the USA and its exemplary credit rating. As we have seen, this faith can be stretched somewhat. The Fed could choose to add to the supply of money and dilute the value of that dollar. You have no influence in that decision. In fact, the USA has tripled the supply of its money over the past decade.[6] When interest rates go down, the cost to borrow a dollar becomes less. At the moment, borrowing a dollar has never been cheaper. Adding substantially to the National Debt will also weaken and devalue a currency: something that the USA has been doing on a grand scale for the past decade. Now compare this scenario with gold. When you own an ounce of gold there is never any danger of counter-party risk. There can be no claim against it. Its value is only ever determined by one consideration: the price someone is prepared to pay for gold on a particular day.

Another inescapable problem with fiat currencies is that they require relatively few physical and economic inputs when they are produced. This means they have no direct correlation whatsoever with the physical world, or economic realities. The quantity of fiat currencies is therefore decided by central planners, which means that the money supply in fiat currencies

---

6   https://www.richdad.com/resources/rich-dad-financial
     -education-blog/april-2012/when-the-fed-prints-money
     ,-what-impact-does-it-hav

is often a wholly inaccurate reflection of the true trading environment. This is a situation not dissimilar to the one currently impacting the stock market and its spectacular bull run: the value of fiat currencies can be higher at one moment, at another lower, than a sensible appraisal of what that country's economy is producing. Once again, this inbuilt vulnerability in the system can either artificially stimulate, or depress, economic activity, depending upon how much currency is created and distributed. Price stability can never ever be reached with fiat currencies.

It is inevitable that fiat currencies become increasingly untethered from reality over time, since they are only ever loosely linked with it. In addition to their distance from physical and economic inputs, they are also pulled around by the actions of each and every one of us. Any economy is the aggregation of the actions of millions of independent individuals and it is impossible to predict, or understand, the results of this until well after the event. Only then is it possible to see whether planning was accurate or inaccurate, in retrospect. Sadly, this can often be through experiencing financial disasters such as credit tightening, recessions, the bursting of large price bubbles and economic collapses.

So, when are fiat currencies at their most vulnerable? It is, without a doubt, in debt-based financial environments, which pretty much sums up most of the Western world right now. Fiat currencies decrease in purchasing power when more currency is produced, as it has been for the last ten years. The depreciation means that the currency has to be continually propped up, or inflated, or the economy that is relying on it will start to deflate, at which point it will become more difficult to service the existing debts and they will grow larger. This propping-up adds to price instability and economic volatility.

What happens, then, when fiat currencies lose their value? Where do investors traditionally turn when it all goes wrong? Yes: gold. The long-term value of gold only tells half the story of its credentials as a wealth preserver. Every time there is a financial crisis, the value of gold soars. People rush to buy gold because its value has never simply disappeared, unlike the value of many household names.

Gold is more than just a reliable bolthole in tough times, though. It is dependable. As the value of fiat currencies like the dollar and the pound continue to erode, it becomes much more difficult to identify the true value of labour or goods. Government meddling with fiat currencies to prop up ailing economies means that currencies are a wholly unreliable measuring stick. After a decade of QE, QT and a bull market in the stock exchange, it is getting harder and harder to know the true value of anything. The only reliable way to identify the true value of wages, goods or commodities is to look into the past and compare their historical prices with gold or silver. The methodology is not completely fool proof, granted, since productivity gains for certain goods can substantially reduce prices, but it should give a fairly good approximation since precious metals have never fallen out of demand and so their purchasing power has remained remarkably stable over long periods. A couple of thousand years ago in Rome, an ounce of gold would have bought you a toga and some leather sandals. Today, that same weight of gold would be enough for a smart Italian suit and shoes. To me, that sums up the power of gold. It does not make you rich: it *preserves* your wealth. No other asset does this better.

To make this fair, let's make a similar comparison with the British pound, which has had fiat status for longer than any other currency circulating today. We cannot stretch back to Roman times: the pound has only been around in its current form since 1694, when the Bank of England was established (granted, the pound as a unit had been around since Anglo Saxon days).[7] You might think the enduring pound has been pretty steady and reliable, but it hasn't. In 1694, the pound was defined as the value of 12 oz of silver. In 2019 it is worth less than 1/200 or 0.5% of its value in 1694. Turn that on its head and that means the pound has lost a terrifying 95.5% of its value. You would definitely need to

---

7 www.intriguing-history.com/bank-of-england-history

downgrade your sartorial expectations in the Italian suit department.

Ah, you may say, but the price of gold goes up and down too. The point is, though, the price of gold does not actually do that. It is the frame of reference that changes. To understand this, you need to view gold as a counting device. It is the currencies that are fluctuating, not the gold. Thus, if the dollar price of gold rises from $1,200 an ounce to $1,350 an ounce, you might see this as the gold price going up, but what actually happened was the dollar went down. It used to cost you $1,200 to buy an ounce of gold and now you will need to pay a further $150. If you spend $1,200, you will take home less gold for your money. A strong dollar means a weaker dollar gold price, while a weak dollar means a higher dollar gold price. Buyers who believe the dollar is set to get weaker might want to consider putting more gold in their portfolio.

In every instance, gold passes the test of time. It's rare, reliable and dependable and, most importantly, the only currency to retain its value.

FOUR

History Speaks – What Drives The Price Of Gold

Investment in gold is not a shot in the dark. It is a consistent strategy that has paid dividends time and again through history. When times get tough, wise investors consistently turn to gold to protect their wealth against economic crises or inflation. In such times they have been rewarded with soaring prices in return.

If you had invested £100,000 in equities and bonds at the turn of the millennium and received the maximum possible return by watching the markets like a hawk and reinvesting dividends, that investment would be worth roughly £320,000 today.[1] If, however, you'd put your £100,000 into gold in January 2000, that investment would now be worth around £450,000.[2] If you compare £320,000 to £450,000, which outcome would you prefer?

The rise in gold prices is not linear. Indeed, gold's price history has had some significant ups and downs. Dramatic changes in price have been fuelled by central bank buying, inflation, geopolitics, monetary policy, equity markets and more. When weighing up a decision to invest in gold, it is helpful to know what influences price changes. To assist you, I have laid out the five main triggers for gold price surges below:

1. **Financial crises/military conflict:** In uncertain times, investors look to gold. The uncertainty can be economic, or conflict-led, but the result is the same. (We will look at the short- and long-term impact of conflict in greater detail in

---

1   *Gold is a Better Way*, Adam Baratta
2   *Gold is a Better Way*, Adam Baratta

chapter 5.) At a time of crisis, investor capital will flow out of stocks and bonds and into gold.

2. As a rule of thumb, the bigger the upset, the greater the gold price surge. During the three-year period around the global credit crunch, gold reached a peak of $1,895 an ounce, almost 90% above where it was at the start of that period. There have been plenty of other surges throughout history too, and these rapid increases are always connected to significant events and times of uncertainty.

3. **Inflationary pressures:** During the 1970s, gold prices rose 18-fold when inflation reached peacetime records and interest rates soared. When inflation began to edge up once again in the early 2000s, and interest rates were raised markedly in the USA and UK, gold outperformed both stock and bonds and nearly doubled in price. It is worth noting that even though inflation has eased back today, it has still eaten into the purchasing power of cash and is continuing to have an impact.

4. One of the biggest drivers of gold value is **movement in currency values**. Since gold is priced in dollars, the Greenback can have a significant impact on the price of gold anywhere in the world. A weaker dollar can make the precious metal relatively less expensive for buyers outside the USA and a stronger dollar has the reverse effect.

5. **Government debt and deficits:** There is a direct correlation between National Debt and the price of gold. Again, let us look at the USA and the dollar's close correlation with the gold price. From 1987 to 2002, when the US National Debt topped $3.4 trillion,[3] the price of gold averaged around $340 per ounce.[4] During the brief period when the US government enjoyed a budget surplus in the years immediately before the millennium, there were successful efforts to reduce the National

---

3   All figures for the US National Debt quoted in this paragraph are taken from www.treasurydirect.gov/govt/reports/pd/mspd/mspd.htm

4   All gold prices in this paragraph are taken from www.jmbullion.com/charts/gold-price

Debt. The price of gold dropped to $270 per ounce during that period. The reduction in National Debt was short-lived. Indeed, National Debt not only returned to its former levels, but soared past them to $15 trillion by 2011. When this happened, the gold price surged alongside it, finishing up at $1,500 an ounce. During this period, the gold price passed $1,900 per ounce at one stage, which was taken to mean gold was over-valued. Today, when the US National Debt stands at a record-breaking $22 trillion, and the gold price is at around £1400, gold is currently undervalued.

6. **Stock market enthusiasm:** Gold usually moves in the opposite direction to the stock market. When equity investors get cold feet, and confidence drops, they often turn to gold. When confidence is strong and there is an appetite for risk, the money flows away from gold.

You may be wondering who decides the price for gold. The answer is that the gold price is primarily set in financial markets, just like the prices for other metals, and for stocks and bonds. In fact, around 15,000 times more gold is traded in financial markets than there is physical gold in the trading process. Contracts are settled in cash, not gold.

Supply and demand for physical gold has very little impact on the price. Instead, the financial market price is set between the London Bullion Market Association (LBMA) banks and COMEX (the US Commodity Exchange) in Chicago. COMEX is one of the biggest, most established, derivatives markets in the world, while the LBMA is steeped in history and has some rather eccentric rules. Gold traders in the London Metals Exchange have to keep one heel touching their seat at all times when operating in the trading ring, for example. There are Asian gold exchanges too, and their importance is growing, but they are still a long way from matching the prominence of the UK and US markets.

What is it that the gold traders are looking out for? It is well known that gold's biggest strength is in preserving wealth during uncertain times. Gains of 150% are not uncommon and if this is against a backdrop of a collapsing stock market, it is easy to see why gold is so attractive at these times. This is why we are seeing gold prices edging up again. As the reality of the weakness of the global economy starts to sink in, with bonds, equities and other financial assets starting their inevitable decline, andthe weakening dollar and inflation starting to increase, it is inevitable that gold will get the attention of investors and be in the spotlight once again. Think of the five drivers we have just discussed. When other assets have been manipulated, heavily inflated and misrepresented, gold comes into its own. Analysts are predicting that values will soar once more, as investors and commodity traders shift into the safe haven of gold.

Anyone weighing up gold as an investment, possibly by diverting their money away from traditional stocks and bonds, might be wondering if it is prudent to own gold as a performing investment as well. Is it possible that it will outperform other investments in your portfolio? Many gold advocates prescribe 'rules of thumb', for example that investors should always hold

10% of their investable wealth in gold. It is the only way to keep your wealth robust in good times and in bad. However, while gold is a good bet for safety, it will not make spectacular gains at a time when the rest of the market is performing well and economies are relatively buoyant. While gold markedly outperforms other investments during crises, often its price does not change significantly the rest of the time. Indeed, it often struggles to keep up with the stock market. However, if you are still keen to speculate on the gold price, there are opportunities. This is particularly so for investors outside the USA.

American investors benefit least from owning gold. Why? Because of differences in currency values. As I have already stated, gold is priced in dollars. The price is then converted into local currencies to get the local gold price. Even if the dollar price is steady, fluctuating exchange rates can mean fluctuating local prices.

There are, of course, many potential outcomes here. If gold is going to form part of your investment strategy, careful thought needs to be given to how changes in the value of your domestic currency will impact the prices at which you can buy and sell gold in various scenarios. Currency fluctuation may offset losses, but it might also add to them. It is not unlike the variables that impact the traditional currency markets.

There are several variables at play that can combine to produce a variety of outcomes as an investor outside the USA. If, for example, the price of gold and your currency rise, you will profit from gold, but lose money on the exchange rate. Alternatively, if your currency dropped, but the price of gold still rose, you would profit from gold *and* the exchange rate. At the other end of the scale, if the gold price fell and so did your currency, you'd lose money on the gold price but make money on the exchange rate. The worst-case scenario is where gold prices fall and your currency rises, in which case you'll lose money on both.

If you look at these variables, it is possible to see why gold is such a good bet during a financial crisis, particularly for those outside the USA.

At times like this, the dollar usually surges, while all other currencies sink. The combination of the pound sinking versus the dollar and gold's price going up means a good return. It is clear that a crisis is fairly good for an American investor in gold, but they will not get any additional benefit if the dollar goes up too. However, the value of gold generally rises more rapidly than that of the dollar during crises.

Whatever your starting point, or location, gold is the canny investment in difficult times.

FIVE

Gold And Conflict

We live in uncertain times. Right now, the threat posed by Islamic State continues to destabilise the Middle East, there are rising tensions between the USA and North Korea and Iran, ongoing conflict between Israel and Palestine, and an escalating political stand-off between Russia and the West. Meanwhile, many other regions such as Libya, Egypt and the Horn of Africa are struggling to weather the storm of increasing political tensions. Viewed purely from the perspective of gold, what are the implications? After all, the prices of other assets are affected by war, or even just the threat of conflict. Wars are synonymous with printing money and accelerated government spending. It would come as no surprise if investors turned their attention to gold and other precious metals whenever conflict looms.

History shows that this assumption is often correct. The late 1970s saw numerous upheavals: the Iranian Revolution in 1978, the Iran-Iraq war in 1979, the Soviet Union's invasion of Afghanistan in December 1979 and the Iranian hostage crisis at the US Embassy in Tehran in the same year. The markets responded with heightened activity in gold prices. The price rose 23% in 1977, 37% in 1978 and 126% in 1979. On 4 January 1980, gold prices hit what was an all-time high in inflation-adjusted dollars: $850.[1] In today's money, that would mean more than $2,400 an ounce. What pushed the price to that height were the prolonged global instability thanks to these successive conflicts, US inflation

---

1   www.theguardian.com/business/2010/sep/17/gold-price
     -timeline

at a dizzying 13%[2] and a growing lack of faith in governments and the currencies they backed.

Another record peak was achieved after another lengthy period of uncertainty. The peak in this instance was a gold price that reached $1,920 and it came in 2011,[3] after several successive Arab Spring revolutions descended into civil war and Greece was brought to a standstill by a general strike in a backlash against uncompromising austerity demands from the EU.

The two fastest one-month gains in the gold price during the last thirty years also coincided with prolonged uncertainty. The first spike saw a 25% rise in the gold price in October 1999. While the price rise coincided with a coup in Pakistan and Russian apartment bombings that killed 293, the real reason that gold soared was closer to home. The markets had fixated on the price of gold for weeks; it fell to a low of $251 in August 1999, based on worries that central

---

2   www.in2013dollars.com/1980-dollars-in-2017?amount
    =850
3   www.telegraph.co.uk/finance/personalfinance/investing
    /gold/11014933/The-seven-drivers-of-the-gold-price.html

banks and mining companies were reducing their gold reserves, selling off their stocks in forward markets to protect against falling prices. When an agreement was struck between fifteen European central banks to limit gold sales, gold rapidly soared to a two-year high of $338.

The second rapid gain came in May 2006. This time, the price of gold rose by 23% during a period of heightened tension as the USA was pressing in the UN for sanctions against Iran. The long, bitter war of words that surrounded this dispute had pushed up the price of crude oil, while the dollar had weakened to an eleven-month low against the euro. Economic growth was picking up but still sluggish and erratic. When Iran announced its uranium enrichment programme, in defiance of the West, the price of commodities shot up. Gold, which had already been rising steadily thanks to rising demand and limited supplies, spiked.

Where the gold price spikes thanks to exceptional events, the spikes are usually in *anticipation*, rather than a response to an event. This is perhaps why those spikes can often be short-lived, particularly if the conflicts that they coincide with are also fairly short-lived. A good example would be the Falklands crisis of 1982. Gold leapt by 12% during the first two weeks of the conflict, but the deeper, medium-term trend remained downward. The initial gains in April of that year were erased within weeks as soon as it became clear the war would be over quickly. Indeed, the price hit a three-year low after the British re-took Port Stanley in June.

Gold prices also jumped when Iraq invaded Kuwait on 2 August 1990. The leap was $10, up to $380. That proved to be short-lived, too. In fact, that $380 proved to be an average price: the price briefly spiked at $412, then softened to $365 by the end of the war seven months later. After that, gold continued its downward trend as disinflation took hold.

Another key event to consider is the attack on the United States of 11 September 2001. Gold prices initially surged in anticipation of war and there was a further upward trend following the US invasion of Iraq in 2003. Once more, though, as soon as a degree of confidence built

up that the war would be short and successful, gold quickly reverted to its pre-war value.
As a rule, gold prices generally correct once
investors have fully assessed the situation and
considered all the ramifications.

For those observers who are keenly watching
the current geo-political situation and want to
weigh up for themselves whether or not this
is a good time to invest, what are the signs
to watch for? As we can see from the historic
snapshot of some significant global conflicts
from the past half-century listed here, while
initial uncertainty can move gold prices, this
situation generally does not last once investors
are fully appraised of the situation. There are
times when the gains can take hold for longer,
however, and this is where factors interact. As
well as the threat of imminent conflict, there
must also be concerns over economic growth
and a conviction in the markets that governments and central banks are not taking the right
course of action. If you look back on the crises
listed above, the times when the price gains
were most rapid and enduring coincided with
wider economic concerns.

This scenario works the opposite way, too. The gold price tumbled in late 2016, following President Donald Trump's surprise election victory. Although there was some degree of sabre-rattling over conflicts in Iraq, there were also raised expectations among investors that the new president would introduce policies that would lead to inflation, higher interest rates, a stronger dollar and better returns on investment.

As outlined at the beginning of this chapter, we are currently facing tensions all over the globe and investors are, without a doubt, getting jittery about what might unfold in numerous potential conflicts. On monetary policy, administrators have been intervening for some time and there is evidence that more measures are under way to protect falling economies. In the USA, a combination of the dollar being under pressure with fears that the US economy may fall into recession has left the Federal Reserve poised to react. The Fed has already voiced fears that the trade war between the USA and China is weighing heavily on the economic health of the country and that the needle might need to be moved on monetary policy. Investors have already priced in a rate cut of 25 base points, but there have been rumours that it could be double that. When interest rates are lowered, demand for gold increases. As previously noted, bond yields and gold prices are inversely correlated. Falling bond yields make non-interest-bearing investments such as gold relatively more attractive for investors since the opportunity cost of holding gold reduces.

Elsewhere, there is no denying that the world is in a mess economically. Several countries are well known to be on the brink of defaulting on their debt, including Greece, Spain, Portugal and Italy. Many others, including the UK, USA, Japan and France are in precarious debt situations. These debt crises will not be solved quickly and certainly not without a great deal of pain and turmoil. Meanwhile, on a more immediate, day-to-day level, stocks and shares, currencies and the property market are showing early signs of under-performing, or at least faltering. Once again, this all has to be taken alongside the numerous threats of looming conflicts around the world.

Hardly surprisingly, there are already ample indications that investors are looking to diversify their investment portfolios and turning to gold. In July 2019, the price of gold rose to a six-year high of $1,439, representing a 12% increase in just two months and topping off the longest stretch of weekly gains since 2011.

Investment dollars and pounds will always flow to where they believe they can achieve the greatest return. Sometimes, when markets collapse, the best investors can expect is a safe haven where their money loses the least. This is not the case with gold in crisis periods. Investors who hold gold when there is a combination of conflict worries and economic instability often see consistent gains.

SIX

The Time To Invest In Gold Is: Now

The number one question for any investor who has made up their minds to own gold is: when is a good time to buy it? After all, they will want to be sure that the price of gold will outpace other investments. In this case, we are viewing the impetus for owning gold as being over and above pure wealth preservation. We are looking at investing in gold for gains.

As we saw in chapter 5, living in uncertain times is not by itself reason enough to switch to gold. The threat of conflicts does have an impact on price, but it is often short-lived. No, key to the strength of gold as an investment is what is going on in the rest of the economy. The most important indicator that the economy is in very big trouble indeed is a recession.

History shows we experience a recession every seven to eight years or so. One of the factors defining a recession is a 20%, or greater, drop in stock prices, although the average is actually around 35%. The 2008 recession became etched in all our memories partly because of the precipitous 57% drop in the markets, which ended some of the globe's best known, established finance houses, as well as scores of other, unrelated businesses. The recession before that, in 2000, saw stock prices drop by 47%. As the current bull run continues into its eleventh year, with no apparent signs of abating, the point to remember is: it won't go on forever. There *will* be another recession. And, without a doubt, when the fall happens, it will be big and it will be painful.

The sensible question to ask is: when are we going to be plunged into recession? After all, as everyone keeps telling us, we live in the era of data. Organisations hold information on our every move, billions, or more probably trillions, of data points. Plus, smart data analytics and artificial intelligence can crunch all that data and predict pretty much anything. *So, clever machines*, you might ask, *when are we going to face the negative vortex of a collapsing economy?*

The short answer is: no one can really say with any accuracy exactly when a recession will hit us. The absolute certainty that a recession will occur is as far as we can go for now. You may have noted a number of differing views on timing already. Of all international premiers, President Trump has been (perhaps predictably) the most buoyant about the prospects for the US economy, loudly proclaiming that it is 'doing great', even 'terrific'. Other observers, though, have been cautious. Ray Dalio, the well-known hedge fund billionaire, has stated that the probability of a recession as soon as 2020, is close to 70%.[1] Why have we failed to

---

1   www.nypost.com/2018/02/22/ray-dalio-sees-70-percent
-chance-of-us-recession-by-2020

reach consensus, though? Why, despite all this data, do we know so little?

Issues with data

The issue with the data is not the data itself. It is more to do with how we analyse and interpret it. One serious problem when it comes to pinpointing the exact date of any looming slowdown is, we can only draw on what has happened in the past. The figures we have on growth (or otherwise) are all from past events, such as the last quarter's employment figures or property indexes. These are called 'lagging' indicators. Lagging indicators are not always helpful when trying to predict future or 'leading' trends. Some leading indicators are taken to be a better tool for predicting slowdowns. Analysts often cite what is known as an 'inverted yield curve' when it comes to forecasting downturns. This is what happens when ten-year bond yields dip below those of two-year bonds. Put simply, the thinking is that if long-term returns are lower than short-term ones, growth is likely to slow in the near future. It is worth pointing out that the inverted yield curve is not a magic spell. While every recession since 1945, without fail, has seen an inverted yield curve appear such curves have also appeared during this period but not been followed by recession.

None of which solves the problem of pinpointing when the recession will occur. The not-terribly-satisfactory rule is that you need to combine clues from both lagging and leading indicators, together with your own judgement. Gather as much information as you can and then weigh up where you believe the economy is going. It is not an easy thing to predict. Right now, the economy *seems* to be doing OK, despite the inversion of that tell-tale yield curve. Take the American economy as an example, since the dollar is still reserve currency and still defines the price of gold and, as pointed out earlier, the present administration is very vocal in its proclamation that the US economy is all-but bullet proof. The consensus among professional economists is that it will continue to grow at a rate of around 2.6% per annum, which is down from last year's 2.8%, but not an unrespectable figure.[2] The 2020 forecast is 2.1%, which is again not too worrying.

Other outwards signs are also positive, or at least seem to give no cause yet for alarm. Consumer spending is driving the US economy and real-person consumption is showing 2.4% year-on-year growth in 2019, compared with 2.6% in the last quarter of 2018. Jobs figures appear promising too, with the average increase in overall numbers employed expected to be 184,000 in 2019, and 139,000 in 2020. Yet dig a little deeper and there are a number of worrying trends. Something that has alarmed many analysts are clear signs that the housing market is slowing. Investment in residential property is forecast to drop 1.3% from 2019 levels in 2020. The drop is predicted to be particularly acute among the lower tiers of housing stock, as many first-time buyers find themselves simply priced out of the market. We could well have reached the tipping point at which the prolonged period of soaring house prices will finally strangle the

---

2   Data in this section is taken from www.fortune.com/2019 /06/04/next-recession-2020-predictions

market, leading to a long-anticipated downturn in house prices.

There is more. Economists are starting to take escalating protectionist trade policies very seriously indeed and are actively factoring in long-term implications. A survey of more than fifty economic forecasters by the National Association for Business Economics found that just 15% of the forecasters expected a US recession by the end of 2019, but 60% of them forecast a recession by the end of 2020, predicting it will most likely be in full swing by November, following the US presidential election. It should also be said that such timing could not be worse. With an ever more polarised political climate in the USA, the beginnings of a slowdown in growth just ahead of the election would be a disaster on every level. Who would put money on the Democrat-controlled House passing any spending bill that would stimulate the economy in that fevered campaigning environment? Anyone expecting any sort of bipartisan impetus towards intervention via proactive fiscal measures will, more than likely, be in for a disappointment.

As worrying as the situation looks in the USA, it is equally concerning elsewhere. Indeed, it has been said the short- and medium-term prospects are far worse for the European Central Bank and the Bank of Japan. In both cases, the starting point of inflation is lower and policy rates are still negative. There is less room for manoeuvre when things do turn sour.

There is always an element of self-fulfilling prophecy in these situations. The more voices that express uncertainty over international markets and domestic trade policies, the more inclined will be both company bosses and consumers alike to rein in spending. Their hesitancy to invest will further fuel the slowdown in economic growth and could even provoke a recession sooner than expected.

The next obvious question is: how bad will the downturn be? Will we experience another 57%+ drop in the market? The experts are predicting that the next recession will not be *as bad* as the 2008/9 financial crisis. However, it will be severe. Once the market flips and begins to head downwards, it is highly likely that the 'bear market' will be as exaggerated as the preceding bull market.[3] Given that valuations have become absurdly high, it is not inconceivable that the market could drop by between 40 and 50%.

Governments' room for manoeuvre

What is equally, if not more, worrying is that the recession could very well last longer than usual because of all the resources that went into fighting the effects of the previous crisis. Governments simply have fewer tools and less resources on hand to fight any fresh downturn. From a monetary policy perspective, central banks will be unable to rely on QE to the same degree as before. While it could undoubtedly provide some short-term stimulus, the efficacy of QE as a long-term solution has already been called into question. Politicians have already

---

3   A 'bear market' is where the price of securities falls 20% or more from recent highs amid negative market sentiment.

spoken out against the scale and duration of recent programmes and it is unlikely that QE will ever again be used to the same extent that it was in response to the 2008 crisis. To do so could completely destroy confidence in the system. Similarly, with interest rates already at record lows, there is almost nowhere for them to fall. In southern Europe austerity policies are still in place. How do you tighten an already pinched economic outlook? In Spain, Portugal, Greece and Italy in particular, it is highly unlikely there are any opportunities for any sort of fiscal tightening. This, in turn, will increase concerns about the long-term viability of the eurozone, along with all the political manoeuvring and fall-out that goes with it.

Credit markets will almost certainly be hit very hard indeed. This is thanks to the record levels of debt, compared to GDP. Historically, debt levels of 90% of GDP are linked to significantly higher levels of inflation.[4] When the debt:GDP ratio hits, or passes this level, inflation rises

---

4   www.heritage.org/budget-and-spending/report/how
     -the-united-states-high-debt-will-weaken-the-economy
     -and-hurt

to around 6% per annum. When debt levels are below 90%, you can expect inflation to be around the 0.5% to 2.5% mark. In the USA, debt stands at a ratio of more than 105% of GDP and rising.[5] The US ratio is higher than elsewhere, but it is leading the trend. In Spain, for example, the level is 99%.[6] The Federal Reserve and Washington are working on resolving the issue, as are the heads of other countries looking to resolve their own debt:GDP ratios, but one possible measure, which is devaluing the currency to reduce the debt burden, has other negative implications. Whatever happens, if the issue is not properly addressed by the time the next recession hits, the fallout will be significant.

There is no use looking East for help, either. During the 2008 recession China was a major source of global stimulus thanks to a massive programme of credit easing and infrastructure spending. It is hard to imagine the last recession could have been worse, but without China that

5   https://howmuch.net/articles/national-debt-of-the
     -united-states
6   www.ceicdata.com/en/indicator/spain/government-debt
     --of-nominal-gdp

would certainly have been the case. But not next time. China has, until recently, been working to deleverage its economy and the growth in its debts over the past decade has rivalled some of the largest debt bubbles in history. When we enter a global recession, the Chinese are unlikely to have resources to deliver anything close to the same stimulus as before, even if it manages to avoid its own hard landing.

When is the right time?

Whatever happens and whenever it happens, investors should be prepared for a steep decline in the economy. But when is the right time to turn to gold? After all, we are still, technically at least, in the midst of a boom. Interest rates remain at record lows. Both stocks and bonds have been on a bull run that has lasted more than a decade, having produced gains of more than 300% since 2009. No investor wants to take the gamble of taking the profit and walking away while there is still the prospect of making good gains.

Comparing such decisions to gambling is interesting, but I would turn the comparison on its head and ask: can you afford to gamble with your financial future? At the risk of stretching the comparison too far, consider how a casino makes its money. The house always wins because every gambler has a limit to what they can lose, but few ever limit what they can win. Many a punter who has had good luck will keep putting their chips back on the table until much or all is swallowed up, rather than walking away and taking their profits. Likewise, many investors.

With your investment portfolio, you need to set limits to what you are prepared to invest, to lose and, crucially, to what you win. All investors need the discipline to take the profit they planned to make and then walk away, in order to protect it for the long term. In a volatile, boom-and-bust market, fuelled by massive debt, you need to manage your investments actively. Set limits to your upside. Keep in mind that these assets can devalue at a tremendous rate when the market does, eventually, collapse, taking with them most, if not all, of your profit, and that this will probably happen quicker than you will ever be able to react.

It is possible that you will miss out on a short period of boom times. If you do, though, you will be in good company. Warren Buffett has repeatedly walked away at what might have seemed an odd time to do so. In 1999, when the Dot Com Bubble was at its height, he took his money off the table and left. By leaving when the market was 12% below its high-point, he missed the final days of the party. He also missed losing most of what he had gained over the previous few years, when the market collapsed almost overnight. Needless to say, he went back in and bought dot com stocks at a substantial discount when everyone was heading in the opposite direction, trying to salvage what they could. Buffett did the same again in February 2007, moving out of the markets and placing nearly 40% of his portfolio into a cash position. Once again, most of Wall Street stayed until the last second of the party, with stocks travelling a further 14% higher after Buffett had left. Although Buffett missed this last hurrah, he was left with enough money to be able to go back in and bail out Bank of America, buying their stock at a few cents on the dollar. He also bailed out Goldman Sachs at a discount, and played a big part in stopping AIG Insurance from disappearing without trace. All this was possible because he took his cash out in good time.

As noted at the close of chapter 5, there are already signs that numerous investors have seen the writing on the wall and are heading towards the exits, or at least towards the safe haven of gold. This, in great part, is why the gold price is gradually nudging northwards.

There is also the law of supply and demand to consider in this environment. There is a finite amount of gold available and the potential for its value to increase substantially has not gone unnoticed. China, which currently has an output of 455 metric tons a year (overtaking South Africa as the largest gold producer in the world),[7] is now also an aggressive acquirer of

---

7   www.focus-economics.com/blog/gold-the-most-precious
    -of-metals-part-3

gold. In 2016, China imported gold worth $64 billion, while exporting gold worth just $1.2 billion.[8]

South Africa, once the dominant force in gold mining, has seen new discoveries occur less and less frequently. The gold that was easiest to find and extract has already been taken out of the ground. Even when new sources are found, it can take years for a gold mine to begin producing new gold supplies in any quantity (or quality). Meanwhile, the USA holds the greatest quantity of gold in its reserves, but the amount has been virtually unchanged since the beginning of the century.[9]

What all this means is: demand for gold far outweighs the supply and that trend is only going to get more acute. As supplies dwindle and demand rises, gold prices will increase. It is the basic economic rule of supply and demand.

---

8   www.fool.com/investing/2017/08/05/the-worlds
    -5-biggest-gold-exportersimporters.aspx

9   www.usfunds.com/investor-library/frank-talk/top-10
    -countries-with-largest-gold-reserves/#.XYix2S-ZPUI

Anyone weighing up their gold investment will inevitably give some thought to how high that price might go. Gold-market expert Adam Baratta, the author of *Gold is a Better Way*, has predicted that gold will more than double in value in the next three to four years, to more than $2,600 per ounce. His argument is based on comparing the price of gold in 2008, when the US national debt topped $10 trillion, to the country's current national debt – in excess of $20 trillion. He then looked at gold in the same period: more than a decade ago, gold was at $1,000 an ounce, compared with around $1,400 today. The money supply has increased to six to seven times its 2008 value through borrowing and QE, and Baratta's view is that a fair price for gold today should be nearer $6,000 to $7,000 per ounce. By this reckoning, it could even hit $10,000 per ounce in the next decade.[10] For the Dow Jones index to keep up with that growth, it would need to soar to 200,000 in the same period.

---

10   *Gold Is a Better Way*, Adam Baratta

Baratta is not the only gold expert who is expecting significant price increases. Jim Rickards, who has written his own book on the precious metal, *The New Case For Gold*,[11] also projects a price of $10,000 per ounce. Leigh Goehring, a respected commodity trader who has been investing exclusively in oil, gas and precious metals since the early 1980s, goes even further. Goehring believes gold prices will spike as high as $13,000 an ounce.[12] Goehring has been proved right, or nearly so, in the past. In the year 2000 he forecast that gold would go to $2,500 an ounce. At the time, the precious metal was at just $250. One decade later, gold sold at $1,900, so he was not far off. Certainly, if you were an investor who bought in at $250 and held on to benefit from such a big leap, you probably would not have quibbled.

It is impossible to say when gold will make its move in response to the perfect storm of current global financial, economic and political threats, let alone the increasing focus on the commodity.

11 Penguin, 2016
12 www.realvision.com/tv/shows/the-jim-grant-series /videos/leigh-goehring

The only certainty is: it will happen. And all the signs point to the fact it will most likely be soon.

The stage is set for the value of gold to make a dramatic move.

Afterword – Certainty In An Uncertain World

Gold is, without a doubt, the ultimate insurance policy. It has proved itself again and again as the right, most profitable, choice at uncertain times. It has remained a steady source of value over hundreds of years, seeing off numerous fiat currencies, triumphing over periods of inflation and even hyperinflation, and remaining unscathed at times of financial, or even political, collapse.

Despite what I hope you will agree are the very convincing arguments I have set out in this book, there will always be detractors. In fact,

I am pretty certain that, even as the economy collapses into the next recession, a large number of these detractors will urge you to stay away from gold. These will be the die-hard, 'buy and hold' investors, who will always stick with the markets come what may. Buying stocks and bonds and holding them is a perfectly good strategy in the right circumstances, but as I have shown here, holding gold comes into its own in exceptional circumstances.

If you feel compelled to explore why, actually, now is the right time to invest in gold, allow me to help. Here are a few answers to the age-old anti-gold arguments I hear again and again.

'Investing in gold is old fashioned. It's a relic from payments systems that operated centuries ago.'

Just because something is old does not make it redundant. Commodities such as concrete, paper and even alarm clocks have been around since ancient times and they are still pretty useful. Granted, there were some faults in the gold standard that dominated world economies in various forms from 1870 until the Second World War. The gold standard suffered from some of the same problems as any fixed-exchange system. Not only can the exchange rate not be adjusted to buffer against external shocks, but also the system attracts speculative attacks. As a result, inflation and economic growth were quite volatile under the gold standard, which was not good for anyone. There is, however, no reason why some sort of derivative gold standard, a hybrid of what went before, could not work well, together with a discretionary monetary policy. Here, central banks could act as a lender of last resort and expand and contract the money supply as and when required to keep things on an even keel. In any scenario, gold still represents a strong component of our global financial systems and many very respected investors and experts agree with this statement.

'There are not enough gold resources to support the financial system.'

There is, indeed, a finite amount of gold. Out of the world's total supply of around 193,472 metric tons of gold, around 33,230 tons are known as 'official gold' and held by central banks, finance ministries and sovereign wealth funds.[1] The criticism that there is not enough gold actually means there is not enough at current prices. It assumes that paper money has a real value, comparable to that of physical gold. In reality, gold can support any amount of international finance and commerce under a gold standard – at a price. This price could be calculated via the simple ratio of physical gold to the money supply. When confidence in paper money is eroded (and a recession will do that), the more likely it is that some sort of derivative gold standard will gain favour as a means to restore confidence in the global economic system.

'The supply of gold cannot be replenished quickly enough to make it a serious player.'

This is an interesting one, especially considering what has happened to our economy thanks to central bank meddling with the money supply through processes like quantitative easing. It is

---

1   www.gold.org/goldhub/data/above-ground-stocks

true that you cannot simply produce more gold, but that is not necessarily a bad thing.

If governments really did feel it prudent to increase their stocks of gold, they would have quite a bit of room for manoeuvre when it came to adding to the official gold supply. As detailed in the previous sub-section of this afterword, the official stocks represent roughly a fifth of the total gold in existence. It would be possible to double, or triple, stocks by buying privately held gold, without making a huge dent in the overall stock of gold. This would not be far different from QE, but it illustrates the point.

In this same context, critics might point out that gold markets are not set up to adequately support inflationary growth. Clearly, GDP is growing faster than they can pull gold out of the ground. There is nothing to say that global economies cannot continue in this way, but if they do there would be a slight deflationary bias in the gold price, which is never a bad thing for both consumers and savers. It certainly seems less damaging, or distorting in the long run, than simply printing more money.

'Gold has no yield.'

Somehow, this has become shorthand for gold is not a viable investment option. It is a widespread misconception, though. In truth, receiving no yield until you sell your holding is exactly why gold is such a necessary part of an investment portfolio.

Yield is derived from risk. Without risk, there is no yield. The money in your wallet does not have yield. The yield comes from putting it into the bank. It then becomes the bank's unsecured liability.

You might believe that the bank is solvent and safe and will absolutely, definitely return your investment at a time of your choosing, paying you interest in the meantime. Except, this is not always the case. In the USA, there were eight bank failures in 2017, five in 2016 and eight more in 2015. There were many, many collapses at the height of the 2008/9 crisis. In Europe, we have seen banks collapse in the UK, Iceland, Cyprus and Greece. All too often, bank depositors have been shown in the most painful way possible that there is a real difference between a bank deposit and actually owning a physical asset. When banks close, it is always a huge shock for anyone who has deposits there; ATMs are closed, cheques are no longer honoured, transfer requests may no longer be accepted (whether or not the bank's website is still up) and, in some cases, depositors have been forced to convert their cash into bank stock.

Next time someone puts forward the 'gold has no yield' argument, turn it on its head. You can certainly get yield from stocks, bonds, rental property and other assets, but in each case there is risk. When a recession hits, and the economy collapses, all of these investments are at risk. With gold, much lower risk, or safety concerns, exist. If you buy an ounce of gold today and keep it for ten years, you will still have an ounce of gold. The dollar price may have changed substantially over that time. In fact, it probably will have. However, your holding will still have some value, even if new gold mines are discovered.

Without wanting to get apocalyptic here, it is worth pointing out that it is now much, much easier for governments and central banks to take measures to correct a currency crisis, no matter how extreme. Thanks to the rise of the cashless, digital society, few people actually rely on physical currency today. We are paid electronically and buy most of our goods with cards, or smart phones or wearable payment devices. Many of us never carry a bank note from one week to the next. Digital wealth is vulnerable, though. Not only is it subject to power cuts, storm damage and exchange collapses, to hackers and online theft, it is also far easier for central authorities to control. At a time of extreme crisis, governments could decree a withdrawal limit at ATMs, regardless of how much you have in your account. A fortune is useless unless you can draw on it. Ultimately, physical assets (like gold) can be traded when banks freeze.

Hopefully those questions will help, if you are in a position where you feel the need to fight your corner. If you really want to look beyond what the detractors say, though, you might also wish to step back and take a wider view. Gold is, without a doubt, gaining attention in the world monetary system. Although, ostensibly, the gold standard was seen off by President Nixon in 1971, it has continued to underpin the global monetary system one way or another, thanks to intentional efforts to stabilise the dollar's value via the gold price. There is even a name for this: the shadow gold standard. This is why the USA has steadfastly hung on to more than 8,000 tons of gold and Germany and the IMF have around 3,000 tons each. It is also why China and Russia are stealthily building up huge stocks of gold, year by year.

One of the key reasons for the prolonged interest in gold is that our governing powers know that, when the next liquidity crisis hits, they have essentially run out of resources to stem the damage. There is a limit to how long central banks can keep printing money without destroying confidence which is already pretty shaky. The only real shelter from the coming storm lies in hard assets and gold is one of the most important of those hard assets.

Just to play out this scenario a little further, consider what will happen at a government level when the downturn inevitably comes. One of the ways that the shadow gold standard is being evaluated is by comparing the amount of official gold each country holds in its reserves with that country's GDP. This gives us important clues as to where the future balance of power might fall. Right now, the centre of gold power lies in the Eurozone nations, where gold is in the region of 4% of GDP. The USA's gold reserves are worth around 2.7% of its GDP and Russia's are worth around 2.7%.[2] And China? Well, that is interesting. China, which is pursuing an aggressive strategy of buying gold, is a little coy (read: downright secretive) about the numbers. Clearly it is concerned that if it did reveal its intentions, it would push up the price. The official figure for China's gold stocks is reported to be around 1,650 tons. However, industry insiders put it at nearer 4,000 tons.[3]

---

2   www.marketwatch.com/story/gold-is-the-pile-of-poker
     -chips-in-the-next-global-crisis-2016-04-05

3   www.moneyweek.com/499249/how-much-gold-does
     -china-have-a-lot-more-than-you-think

Why is this important? China's and Russia's gold:GDP ratios are at least mirroring those of the USA and Europe. When the downturn comes, the globe's powers will come together to decide what needs to be done next. China and Russia, who have until now had a disproportionately small say in international monetary policy, will be in a position to tell the world to listen to them. They will have a seat at the top of the negotiating table. Since gold holds the key to sorting out the mess when other measures such as QE stop working, the world will have no choice but to listen. That in itself will ensure a very, very different economic and political system in the years to come.

If there is an international economic crisis, it is not inevitable that anything like the gold standard of old would be introduced. That is just one of many possibilities that might be considered to restore confidence in the financial system. If we did revert to a version of the gold standard, though, it would need to be decided how the price per ounce of gold will be set. One of the big mistakes made after the First World War, when the gold standard was re-adopted, was to peg it at the pre-World War rate. The money that had been printed to prop up the war effort had a terrible deflationary effect, which in part led to the Great Depression in the 1930s. If we were to have a gold standard today, we would need to protect ourselves against a similar outcome. In such a case, the price would need to be at between $10,000 and $50,000 an ounce. The vast range is because of many variables including the choice of reserve currency, ie whether the price would be based on the dollar or some other currency, the percentage of gold backing it and which countries would sign up to the new system. It is unlikely that the price would go as high as $50,000, but $10,000 is not a wild estimate by any means. Even if some sort of gold standard is not adopted, it is almost certain that dollar prices for gold will increase considerably, as governments battle to restore confidence.

The point to take out of this is: it is not just that gold has always been an investment option. It is poised to become a crucial force in global economics once again. Indeed, behind the scenes, it already is. Powerful governments have staked their long- and medium-term strategies on this.

Smart investors will take heed and invest in gold to protect themselves from the economic downturn that is expected to begin in earnest in 2020. Investing in gold is not just the safe haven, enabling you to protect your wealth. Again and again it has proved itself to be resilient through monetary collapses; but it is the *key* to growing your wealth at a time when everyone else is losing theirs.

Now is a great time to buy gold.

References

Baratta, Adam (2019) *Gold is a Better Way* (Morgan James Publishing, reprint 2019).

Rickards, Jim (2016) *The New Case For Gold* (Penguin).

Warren Buffett Indicator calculator available at www.goldisabetterway.com (accessed 12 August 2019).

Acknowledgements

My journey to understanding the value of gold and learning about its place in the world of finance has been an interesting one. With each new source I have found, or book I have read, I have become more and more fascinated by and convinced about its extraordinary place in our economy. I am afraid I have not kept my excitement to myself, so this is definitely the place to thank my good friends Gary Hirst, Christy Hirst, Adam Matich, Neil Barrett, Jonathan Tiffany and Nat McLay for their patience as they listened to my increasingly long rants about gold. Thanks also for never pulling me up on the fact that I laid out the arguments as though they were all still children. I think this was in part to get things straight in my own head. I am glad I did, too, or this book would never have been written.

Thanks also go to my therapist Nathan Gould, who has been instrumental in helping me on a path of self-discovery.

I would also, of course, like to offer a huge vote of thanks to my wife Claire, who has always taken the time to listen to me and, as a result, has taken the leap of faith to invest our funds in gold. Claire has given me the courage to take on this new chapter of my life and her whole-hearted support has been worth its weight in gold. She has, fortunately, seen the rewards. I would also like to mention my children Niamh and Max. I am hopeful that all I am learning is something I can pass on to them one day, so they can play their part in making the world a better place when they have families of their own.

The Author

 Phil Taylor-Guck's career has been fuelled by curiosity. After starting out in partnership with his dad in a flooring business, Phil, who is known as PTG, quickly discovered an entrepreneurial flair and an insatiable curiosity about finding a better way of doing things. His ideas helped quickly expand the business and he moved on to create his own supply chain and new technology to extend the business opportunities. This led PTG on to creating his own investment group and since doing so he has invested in international

companies which work in technology, venture capital, private equity and real estate. A hunger to learn more about commodities, and the technology around the process of delivering them, led him to start to scrutinise the world of finance; a sector he concluded was riddled with fatal flaws. Phil is now CEO of RTK International Holdings, a financial services and commodities trading group, spanning four continents and headquartered in Hong Kong.

www.goldrush2020.co.uk
www.rtkinternational.com
http://taylor-guck.co.uk
🐦 @philtaylorguck